T0197470

Why

ARE YOU HERE

EVELYN ELIZABETH HUGHES-BASS

AuthorHouse™
1663 Liberty Drive
Bloomington, IN 47403
www.authorhouse.com
Phone: 1 (833) 262-8899

Because of the dynamic nature of the Internet, any web addresses or links contained in
this book may have changed since publication and may no longer be valid. The views
expressed in this work are solely those of the author and do not necessarily reflect the views
of the publisher, and the publisher hereby disclaims any responsibility for them.

Any people depicted in stock imagery provided by Getty Images are models,
and such images are being used for illustrative purposes only.
Certain stock imagery © Getty Images.

*Scripture quotations marked KJV are from the Holy Bible, King James Version
(Authorized Version). First published in 1611. Quoted from the KJV Classic
Reference Bible, Copyright © 1983 by The Zondervan Corporation.

This book is printed on acid-free paper.

ISBN: 978-1-7283-7128-3 (sc)
ISBN: 978-1-7283-7127-6 (e)

Print information available on the last page.

Published by AuthorHouse 08/26/2020

authorHOUSE®

CONTENTS

SPECIAL THANKS

Pastor Jerry Warren and Lady Carol Warren and the Saints at Greater
Christ Temple Pentecostal Church and First Pentecostal Church
for your outpouring of love, kindness, and prayers.

Jerrilynn Taylor for editing

BEGIN THE JOURNEY

Life certainly has a particular plan for us to follow. The task is for us to find our own designed purpose. Do we want to discover this purpose? There are ways to pursue the particular plan for our lives. Do we choose the way of the world, which will lead us to a certain kind of satisfaction? There are ways to fulfill our hopes and dreams as we reach our destination. We use the expertise of others in various organizations. We gain knowledge from friends and co-workers. We have been given a choice to live a life of quality and success or to live according to this world system.

I had to face a major problem. I had lived my life for years before I was confronted with questions that I had pondered in my mind. These questions revealed that I had begun the path of life without God. I had endured a period of troubles, trial and tribulations with negative results. I had gotten turned around and was facing unsureness in myself and in others.

My journey, you see, started off wrong. Point blank. I didn't realize it until I had had so many failed situations and plenty of disappointments. These failures left me with issues where I didn't know what to do. I didn't know who to turn to, so I leaned towards alcohol, drugs, clubbing, and sexual activity. In my heart I regretted doing these things, yet I still suffered the consequences. I continued falling on my face and, at times, was crying myself to sleep.

It was as though life had thrown salt in my face. The taste was bitter and fell down constantly in my face. It was a stinging reminder of my past. The salt falls down constantly in my face, reminding me of my past history. This represents the state of my life as I am trying to figure out how I have ended up in this place and how to get on the right track. My mind is puzzled and I'm uncertain. Fears and doubt cloud my mind as I wonder what my turning point is.

I begin to question myself, "Why are you here? There's got to be a better place and way." All I could answer to myself was, "Um…" I have heard different ones speak of a sound mind. How do *I* get there? How do *I* come to a better way of living?

CHAPTER 1

LIVING IN THE STATE OF DENIAL

Being denied can throw you for a loop in life because you can be left with without a sense of direction. While in my own state of denial, my idea of having fun and enjoying life led my way of life until this question arose in my mind, "What is true living?" My mental reflections about living and being loved seemed undefined, that is, with no meaning. Seeking the answer to this question led me to discover that I was on the hard path of disappointments. Yes, I had started off wrong. I was devoted to a world of sin at such a deep level that I didn't realize existed until I began to participate in it. As a result, I developed a taste for sin, and that created an appetite to indulge and enjoy. My lifestyle changed along with my principles. I had wanted to mingle and fit in with the crowd for attention, yet now I am alone, I'm in disarray, and everything is out of control.

I grew up in a small town where love dwelled and many words were spoken about Jesus. My birth family and church family were at church all times during the week. Love was shown throughout the community. My parents gave of themselves through feeding people. If a person needed a place to rest or to sleep, no one was turned down. During my state of denial, thoughts of my childhood brought back to me these sweet memories. This lasted but a short time, and I would yet return to my current lifestyle. This state of denial had taken possession of me through vain thoughts. I didn't think about consequences. I just lived for today.

Even though I did not comprehend what was happening, I do remember having a conversation with myself. It started like this: "I remember when you wouldn't do this…" I would then cry. You see, I was living a life displeasing to the Lord but pleasing to the flesh. I wanted to please me, not others. I was the primary and only objective at this time. The goals for my life were to reach a height of success that satisfied my self-realization. This meant that I could point out the things that I did for myself. At this point I had to concentrate on my desires and wants. I was selfish. Even so, I didn't realize how much I was into myself. I am in a state of denial, which is a dangerous position.

I found myself between a rock and a hard place. I came face to face with consequences that I didn't want to think about. One particular hard place is when I was physically attacked, which then attacked my mental state. You see, I didn't report the attack. I kept it to myself. It was difficult for me to make decisions as my thoughts tossed to and fro. I tried making a concrete decision in this messed up mind of mine. The answers are hard to reach, yet I was still reaching out for success. Even in my state of denial I finally realized that something was wrong with running into a brick wall. Knowing and doing are two different concepts, though. My flesh is in the way, dictating my moves. I didn't realize then that this covering over my body was just that: covering. The real me was inside.

Reflections - Living in the State of Denial

What is your point of view of handling problems you have encountered?

_____

_____

_____

_____

_____

Can you relate your encounter with a positive point of view? If so, how?

_____

_____

_____

_____

_____

Express your feeling through a short poem or a drawing.

_____

_____

_____

_____

_____

Let's read the following scripture and examine the consequence of living in the state of denial.
Luke 15: 11- 24

_____

_____

_____

_____

_____

Encouraging Word

Stay focused and remember who you belong to.

_____

_____

_____

_____

_____

CHAPTER 2

RESISTING THE TRUTH

Truth hurts no matter what is stated, but the key point is to accept the truth. Living by the truth can either change or break a person. In my case, it worked both ways. I had the determination to continue to resist the truth and have life my way. The alternative was that I could keep trying until I was fed up living life my way. This state of mind didn't make any sense, but I was subject to this flesh.

My small-town upbringing did remind me of the real me inside. At times I remembered that, as a child, I listened to the elders in the family. This brought back even more memories of how to live right before God. Back then I had learned what to do and what not to do, and it shaped my mindset at an early age. As an adult I found myself resisting the truth. My mind needed reframing. Thinking back on the lifestyles of the elders placed emphasis on their values, beliefs, behavior, and family conversations.

I was torn between two worlds. This was a weight on my mind because the ways of the world contrasted with my childhood upbringing. I also still didn't want to face the consequences of my choices. I simply did not know what to do. If I did know what to do, I would also know how to go about it.

I could be described as a bull with the force to run down anything. Quite dumb, don't you think? That's how I was, without the Lord in my life. My existence is because of God, but dumb me resisted Him and continued down the path of destruction. The person inside was slowly deteriorating, slowly fading away and losing existence.

Looking back on this time, I have to admit that I didn't see [or don't recall] one person who had success when resisting the truth. I needed to wake up and smell the coffee. I needed a new perspective. I now know that all of our lives have a great effect on others, whether they choose to or decline to follow us. Our steps are being reviewed and recorded just like we are doing a play, playing a role.

Depending on which examples we will follow, the result is a downfall or a higher standard of living that we reach for and conquer. Our decisions are a key component for a better life. What do you consider to be a better life? I pondered this question and came to this conclusion: A better life is when you proceed to the next level of success. You accomplish it by being obedient instead of resistant and when you can receive the truth with a positive mind.

Reflections - Resisting the Truth

Is there value in resisting the truth? If so, or if not, explain your reason.

_____
_____
_____
_____

It was as a child that I listened to my elders. How do you gain one's trust? Explain your response.

_____
_____
_____
_____

What are the consequences of resisting the truth?

_____
_____
_____
_____

Read Daniel 4:28-37. Examine this scripture about resisting the truth.

_____
_____
_____
_____

Working in a group or in a team of two, think of an activity that emphasizes the importance of truth.

_____
_____
_____
_____

Encouraging Word

Choose wisely and seek the mind of God for directions.

_____
_____
_____

CHAPTER 3

BATTLE OF THE MIND

There is a battle going on to defeat our purpose and bring destruction to our existence in this life. We find ourselves wondering which way to turn and who to turn to. This is a true saying, "A battle is going on in our minds." We must speak victory or be defeated. Having a firm grip our beliefs makes this possible. Today, I personally choose victory through Jesus Christ. He is the only one that can give salvation and victory. Keeping in mind that we serve the Lord with our minds, let's do as Philippians 4:8 says and think on "these things": "Finally brethren, whatever things are honest, whatever things are just, whatever things are pure, whatever things are lovely, whatever things are of good report; if there be any virtue, and if there be any praise, think on these things."

There will be a constant battle in your mind if you choose to let it happen. The battle is The Lord's, so we must let go and surrender to Jesus. The best way to be a conqueror is to read the word daily, dedicate our time to doing the will of God, and praying and fasting. The result of these daily activities is a better mindset.

Have you ever noticed how a seesaw operates? It goes up and down or backward and forward in motion. The mind is like a seesaw in the battle of mind control. When my desire to win this battle would decrease, I suffered painful effects. Down. Then The Lord would bring to my memory my family's ethics, which were: "Never give up. Continue to fight for life." Up. A while later I would remember when I gained not rewards for my efforts but setbacks for my failures. Down. This state of confusion can be described as the living dead. We can be walking and breathing but yet dead to knowing our state of existence. Based on evidence, without God we are dead. A small portion of the mind wants to do right, but there is a pull towards destruction, conveying a different message.

With this struggling in the mind, one begins to question the purpose of living. How does a person survive the attacks that constantly weigh on the mind? The answer is inspired through a poem from <u>Listen! The Lord is Speaking</u>.

Obstacles of Life

The obstacles and barriers that come as you are going through
One must hold on to the promises of God and remember his Holy word
To carry us through and pray for enduring power to hold on and go through.
There are many crooks and turns in life, but one chooses the correct path

To follow, the path of righteousness where God is waiting to receive you with open arms.
He's there waiting on you.
Ask him for direction and which way to go.
He shall lead and guide you through
Just ask, now, my daughter.

These are powerful and meaningful words to listen to. These are instructions to be followed. To become an overcomer in this life, we must believe in God for our existence.

The adversary's purpose is to destroy our minds. He wants us to depend on the flesh to govern our minds. Not so! Because we are children of God, let's observe and take heed to the word of God.

Reflections - Battle of the Mind

There is a parallel of being right or wrong. How do you defend yourself in this battle with opposite thoughts?

_____
_____
_____
_____
_____
_____
_____
_____

How do you balance encounters in your life?

_____
_____
_____
_____

When facing the decision of which way to go, how do you draw the conclusion?

_____
_____
_____
_____

Read the book of Jonah and discover how battles in the mind can be resolved.

_____
_____
_____
_____

Encouraging Word

In everything give thanks and keep your mind on Jesus.

_____
_____
_____
_____
_____

CHAPTER 4

CROOKED PATH

There are many paths in this life, the question is, which one will we follow to reach our destination or our purpose in this life? This was a puzzle to me as I traveled along life's journey. Wondering which way to turn was because it was hard to even focus on making a concrete decision. Choosing which way to turn and who to trust and who to believe were hard decisions to make. But life must go on, even though we have problems to encounter.

As I review my past experiences on this path of life, I see myself falling in ditches and holes. I see this world system leading me to destruction. There is a way that seems right, but the end of this road is the path of destruction.

Being saints of God, we must look to Jesus, the author and the finisher of our faith. He knows what is best. He created us from the beginning of time. He is the answer we need to go forth.

Even the word crooked holds evidence of dishonesty in its meaning. The betrayal of your own evil doings will trap you, withholding you from God in your mind. One person's example of a path of life to follow is Noah. Hebrews 11:7 says, "By faith Noah, being warned of God of things not seen as yet, moved with fear, prepared an ark to the saving of his house: by the which he condemned the world, and became heir of the righteousness which is by faith." Noah demonstrated the importance of listening to and following directions from God. His obedience and his willingness to stand on God's word was a straight path to salvation. He didn't see where it was leading, yet he obeyed with the right spirit that pleases God.

This goes to show us that we must have ears to hear God's word. When we follow his instructions, we stay on the path of righteousness. That path is straight but narrow. It will lead to safety in God. Here is another inspired word from <u>Listen! The Lord is Speaking</u>.

Highway to Heaven

The way is narrow but straight
To enter you must be born again
And washed in His blood
Jesus can lead and guide you to heaven
Hearken unto His voice and follow
Obey His holy words.
Only the pure in heart shall enter in
Humble yourself
Learn of Him
And
Enter the highway to heaven

Take a look at this example of detours. This is an example of what your journey may look like.

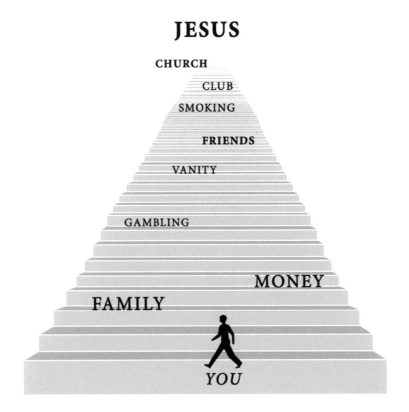

Think is an example of what your journey may look like. Our goal is to reach Jesus and maneuver the path made crooked by the object there to hinder our progress. As you come to each obstacle, think on Proverbs 14:12: "There is a way which seemeth right unto man, but the end thereof are the ways of death."

Think about the word crooked. To receive a clear picture in your mind, imagine walking in unfamiliar territory with a stony, unpleasant pathway. You are walking this path daily because you believe it leads to success in life. However, you find yourself alone and without hope and wondering, "How did I get here?" The next thought that comes to your mind is that you must figure out how to get off this path. It leads to destruction without warning. This path is crooked, so suddenly you are so close to the edge that you fall to depths, into crevices, holes of defeat. You are now ready to remove the deceptions in your mind that brought on this dilemma.

Reflections - Crooked Path

On your journey, recalling your steps to reach your destination, think about the crooked path and how you became an overcomer. What negative or positive elements you gained as you travel, were there benefits?

_____
_____
_____
_____

Read the story of Ananias and Sapphira in Acts 5 and discuss their encounter and their consequences.

_____
_____
_____
_____
_____

Encouraging Words
Trust and depend on Jesus. He will lead you on the straight path of righteousness.

_____
_____
_____
_____
_____
_____
_____
_____

CHAPTER 5

POINT OF DESTRUCTION

There are times in one's life where the wheels of decision turn in no particular direction. With no directions to follow, one then engages in the world system and doesn't have a clue how life's journey will end. You've come to a point of destruction. You come to this point when you are gazing through the eyes of others and viewing life from their stand point. They give their opinion of how you should continue your journey of deception. Sadly enough, their point of view becomes dim and vague the further you walk through life. The reality is that you have been looking past the rules and principles of life and focused on satisfying your fleshly wants and desires.

Really see yourself. See yourself standing among the mass of people you have connected with over the years. See yourself standing among them with your eyes closed. Through them you have been receiving messages of this world system that keep you continuing on the path of destruction. See yourself opening your eyes. You are looking through eyes of deception. Your perception has been flooded by these messages and your mind is entangled. You are in a frozen state of mind and at a standstill, just like ice. There is no movement in the brain or body. Your thinking capability no longer exists. All of this is because you have placed yourself in a web of deception, yet you are still trying to hold on to reality.

See yourself wandering in a daze. Each day comes with doubts and fears. You begin to wonder where is the answer that is needed to break free from this drama. When you seek others to get the answer, you end up with a closed door and no outlet to free your mind. Suddenly, you begin having a conversation with yourself. You have come face to face with the truth that you have been living as though there are no consequences to your actions and lifestyle. You have been looking at life as though you begin and end its journey. "Who do you think you are?" you ask yourself. "Who give you the permission to rule and guide your steps? To perform any task?" More questions come and you speak to yourself from within. "What have I done to land myself in this situation?" Realization finally hits, and true repentance now can overtake you to a state of godly sorrow. At this point you are awake to see clearly. I know this because this was me. We are only actors performing on a stage. We have two choices: serve the Only Wise True God or serve the devil where torment is forever.

Meditate on the following words. May they bring joy, comfort and assurance to hold and never let go.

Before the break of dawn

The Lord arise in each of us

Spreading His joy divine

Within your soul

Giving us the renew of life

With brand new mercy each day

The Lord Our God is within us

Reign with joy divine

Shower of blessings, He has bestowed upon us

Thank you, Jesus, for another day in you

We have victory in you this day.

Let's continue this race with thee

Leading and guiding the way.

Leading and guiding our thoughts, prayers, and our mind to stay upon

thee. And rejoice in thee this day.

That we your people be sold out to thee

Souls being saved, being delivered, and souls returning to you.

Serving you with a glad heart

Giving of yourself to the fullest

Obeying you, serving you with no doubts and fear.

Seeking your face, obeying each word that proceeds out of your mouth.

Being that true witness of you, doing your will.

We are asking this day, guide our prayers that we pray by the anointing

and glory fill the temple this day, that we will lift your name on high.

Giving you reverence and acknowledgement in everything we do.

Looking to thee for you are the author and the finisher of our faith. That

our faith, confidence, and trust go higher in thee. Leaning and depending on

you for our existence in this journey in Jesus name.

These words encourage me to stay on the path of righteousness and not on the path leading me to the point of destruction. I embrace His word daily with assurance.

Reflections – Point of Destruction
Create a story or writing that expresses your emotion at the point of destruction.

_____
_____
_____

Declare how you defeated the destruction before falling over the cliff.

_____
_____
_____

What words or quote inspires you to continue this journey for success?

_____
_____
_____

Read Bible scriptures on how Sodom and Gomorrah were destroyed in Genesis 19:24-29. Give a description of the incident and the cause and effect of destruction.

_____
_____
_____

Encouraging Words
Pray, seek God and mediate on his word before you react.

_____
_____
_____

CHAPTER 6

FACING REALITY

We are creatures of knowledge. As creatures of the human race, we have intelligence, skills and capabilities that allow us to function on a higher level of thinking than all other creatures. Some believe we are conquerors even without God, conquerors with the ability to fulfill challenges with dependence on oneself. This kind of person does not view the pattern of existence of life. He looks at it as a puzzle and fails to properly examine the meaning of life and how it began.

Let's view life from the standpoint of Nebuchadnezzar, the king of Babylon, in Daniel 4:1-37. Pride, self-confidence, and believing we have power beyond God will corrupt and bring damage to your body. In Daniel chapter 4, verses 30 and 31 says, "The king spake, and said, Is not this great Babylon, that I have built for the house of the kingdom by the might of my power, and for the honour of my majesty? While the word was in the king's mouth, there fell a voice from heaven, saying, "O king Nebuchadnezzar, to thee it is spoken; The kingdom is departed from thee." The words spoken to him came to pass; he was with the oxen and eating grass. Verse 33 continues telling what happened: "and his body was wet with the dew of heaven, till his hairs were grown like eagles' feathers and his nails like birds' claws." We must be careful what we speak, how we conduct our lives, and how we treat others.

Thank God for his mercy for us! King Nebuchadnezzar's praise for God is recorded in Verses 34-37: "And at the end of the days I Nebuchadnezzar lifted up mine eyes unto heaven and mine understanding returned unto me, and I blessed the most High, and I praised and honoured him that liveth for ever, whose dominion is an everlasting dominion, and his kingdom is from generation to generation. And all the inhabitants of the earth are reputed as nothing: and he doeth according to his will in the army of heaven, and among the inhabitants of the earth: and none can stay his hand, or say unto him, What doest thou? At the same time my reason returned unto me; and for the glory of my kingdom, mine honour and brightness returned unto me; and my lords sought unto me; and I was established in my kingdom, and excellent majesty was added unto me. Now I Nebuchadnezzar praise and extol and honour the King of heaven, all whose works are truth, and his ways judgment: and those that walk in pride he is able to abase." King Nebuchadnezzar is a primary example of what not to do in life. He faced reality because of God. He saw himself for who he was and learned who is in control.

God has shown us his magnificent power. Let's obey and follow him. There comes a time in life when we must face reality. We must continue with and maintain a sound mind. We need it to function and conduct ourselves as children of the Most High God.

Reflections - Facing Reality

What difficult tasks do you experience in facing reality?

_____

_____

_____

_____

The truth bears pains and regrets in life. What solution solved your issues and helped you to go forth?

_____

_____

_____

_____

Names issues you face now. Name some of the ones you resolved and conquered.

_____

_____

_____

_____

_____

Let's look at David and Absalom in 2 Samuel 15. Explain what deception took place in facing reality.

_____

_____

_____

_____

Encouraging Word
Look and examine before you leap.

_____

_____

_____

_____

_____

CHAPTER 7

LOOKING IN THE MIRROR

I have waited until now to begin my reflections. I can do so only after glancing over my life journey, looking at past events that took place and have brought me to this point. I pondered this question, "How did I get to this point and by what method was I determined to reach my goals?" Reviewing each path that I have followed has led me to know that I needed Jesus the whole time. I didn't realize the importance of Him in my life. Because I have no life without him, my existence is based on him as I go forth.

It is amazing how we can get off track, thinking we have the capacity to proceed in life without God. Oh what a wretched soul I was when I had this idea functioning within myself. Jesus has said plain and clear in John 14:6, "I am the way, the truth, and the life: no man cometh unto the Father, but by me." When I used to read, "I am the way," my curiosity arose, and this thought came to mind, "The way to what?" Then again I used to read John 10:9, "I am the door: by me if any man enter in, he shall be saved, and shall go in and out, and find pasture." What a wonderful statement for me to hold on to! It reveals the love of God in one's life. You learn that you can possess his abundance and the heritage to rest and abide in Him.

Feeding upon His word means that we are receiving the nourishment to sustain us as we travel in this race of life. It is of the utmost importance to look in the mirror and see the image of God. Always remember that we are new creatures in Him. We no longer belong to ourselves but to Him. The bottom line is that we must look like him and not like the cares of this world. Stop trying to fit in with the world's standards but use the Word of God because his standard was designed for your life.

Reflections - Looking in the Mirror

The reflection of a mirror reveals our image. What do you see? Explain your answer.

_____
_____
_____
_____
_____
_____

How do you see yourself and your accomplishments in the next 5 years? If you could revisit your past, what would you change and why?

_____
_____
_____
_____
_____

When Ruth and Naomi traveled together, what image did Ruth see to make a decision to follow Naomi? Let's read Ruth chapters 1-3.

_____
_____
_____
_____
_____

Encouraging Word

See yourself as a winner and a conqueror.

_____
_____
_____
_____
_____
_____
_____

CHAPTER 8

RUDE AWAKENING

There are times in our life when we are faced with consequences and situations beyond our control, and we are caught up in the world system. We are needing help but not knowing which way to turn to solve problems. Then we step off the road of achievement and enter onto the path that leads to no man's land of the world's system. We can play games in the world system for too long. As the result of playing, we get caught up in a web being tied and tangled up and then fall in deep sleep. The world is swallowing us up through vain and popular deception that's pleasing to the flesh, but we don't realize what is happening to us. We are slowly getting deeper in a deep state of denial, refusing to receive the truth and not seeking to know the truth because of the dilemma we are in at this time.

This deep sleep we fall in can also paralyze our mind so that we don't think about the way we live. This web of deception has us trapped, and we cannot face reality. At this point, common sense is not working; the activation of our realization has not kicked in. This is due to the trap of this world system, which has taken over our mind. What a mighty web to be caught up in at this time!

We have been in a deep sleep, a state of denial. Then suddenly, the cracking of dawn, of hope, arises within us! We begin remembering the word of God. We cry out for help and repent of our sins. We thank God for his mercy and kindness toward us. Here is where you will again wonder and ask yourself, "What happened? How did I end up here and at this point in life?" The difference in the answer will be that you now realize and can say, "God gave me another chance to repent and begin a new journey with him and never return to the old state of mind again but live with him and for him."

As I look over the past incidents of my life's journey, God's hand was there all the time, but my spiritual eyes were blinded. Only when I was awakened, the true depth of my existence was revealed. I could then recover my sense of belonging and continue this race. I learned a valuable lesson through experience: don't play the world's games trying to fit in exploring activities such as partying, using alcohol, drugs, organizations with the wrong agenda and representing themselves as Christian organizations. Search the scriptures. Learn the truth and stay in the truth.

Remember, there is a way that seemeth right to man but the end is destruction. Be thankful for the rude awakening. Only God can awake you, so we must cry out to The Lord for help. He can change our heart and mind. People of God, let us wake up and seek the mind of God. Return ye people of God and remember all the great things he's done. Return, Oh return to your first love. He is the one with wisdom, advice, and compassion for others. You are a living example of what you teach, who gave you salvation in his name, Jesus. He will deliver you from the chains that had you bound.

Reflections - Rude Awakening

Picture the clouds of life enclosing around your view. What are some of the entanglements that grasp your attention? Why does this happen?

_____

_____

_____

_____

_____

Imagine falling in a deep sleep and dreaming. Draw a scene describing the events taking place.

_____

_____

_____

_____

_____

_____

List words that describe your rude awakening.

_____

_____

_____

_____

Read 1 Samuel 25. What hasty decision did Abigail make to change the mind set from rudeness to kindness and why?

_____

_____

_____

_____

Encouraging Word

Stay focused and see the true picture.

_____

_____

_____

CHAPTER 9

THE SEARCH IS OVER

Many years passed, as I was wandering from place to place.

I was searching for understanding and for a place in God. Some of my thoughts were "Does God love me or what?! Why am I here? I exist for a reason." I needed these questions answered. I tried many things to resolve them but came to a dead end. Churches of all denominations, men, alcohol and even drugs. In my search for answers, suicide came my way. I was always defeated on every hand. I wanted to do right but couldn't. I cried out, "O Lord! Help me!" but he didn't answer. I would then say, "No one loves me."

One day, the Lord invited me to attend a church which He established and I heard His Holy Word. There stood a vessel of God who showed compassion and was concerned about my soul. The membership expressed the same kind of affection, which I didn't understand. Each time I prayed this prayer unto God, "Lord help me and show me where to go," he replied, "The House of Prayer." I thank God for His sanctuary, where the Holy Ghost dwells and there is the shepherd he chose to feed His flock. To this shepherd I say, "I never will forget your teaching, wisdom, advice, and compassion for others. You are a living example of what you teach. I pray that you continue to be strong in The Lord."

I thank God for my search is over. It is an honor to receive knowledge which was given from God.

Reflections - The Search is Over

There are many steps in this journey. List the steps you took during your search.

_____
_____
_____
_____
_____

To start over again, what changes would you make and why?

_____
_____
_____
_____
_____

What word describes your journey as you searched?

_____
_____
_____
_____
_____

What scriptures strengthen, inspire, and encourage you to continue?

_____
_____
_____
_____
_____

Encouraging Word

Go forth and fulfill your dream.

_____
_____
_____
_____

CHAPTER 10

ENDING THE JOURNEY WITH VICTORY

It is a true statement according to the scripture Ecclesiastes 7:8 "Better is the end of a thing than the beginning thereof: and the patient in spirit is better than the proud in spirit." There is a lesson that was learned during these trials and tribulations that empowered my being to trust in God rather than myself. Without the Lord, I can't make it on this journey in life. I needed him in every step when going forth. When pride and being proud entered my mind to depend upon what I knew, it was revealed to me that I have what I have because of Jesus. Plus, I was challenged with these questions, "Who do you think you are?" "How did you make it this far?" It finally clicked in my mind that it was the hand of the Lord that got me through the years of defeating and fighting this flesh. It was God Almighty who gave me hope and assurance to know the truth is to rest and abide in him.

Learning to let go is a tremendous task to conquer when you are accustomed to controlling life's situations. But through it all, God showed me his love, mercy, and kindness. He turned me around. Now I understand the battle belongs to God. Our God is with us. Isaiah 41:10 says, "Fear thou not; for I am with thee: be not dismayed; for I am thy God: I will strengthen thee; yea, I will uphold thee with the right hand of my righteousness." During this time, I thought I was alone, but he was right there all the time with stretched out hands to help me. I am thankful for his patience with me and never want to take God's love for granted.

There is a bright new day in my life. Now hope, love, mercy and God's precious Holy Ghost dwells with me when I received the baptism in Jesus' name. That was and still is a glorious day to remember and embrace. Since that day there was a healing that took place in my mind, heart and soul. This healing has delivered me and given me the victory so that I can have a forgiving heart for myself and others. It helps me to not point the blame but face reality. I continue to look to Jesus who is the author and the finisher of our faith.

Philippians 3:13-14 says, "Brethren, I count not myself to have apprehended: but this one thing I do, forgetting those things which are behind, and reaching forth unto those things which are before, I press towards the mark for the prize of the high calling of God in Christ Jesus." This scripture is a reminder of my purpose to go forth, not glancing back to bring back old memories and the past. I am a new creature in Christ Jesus. I have victory, being a chosen vessel to serve in the kingdom of God

Printed in the United States
By Bookmasters